Original title:
Orbit of Oddities

Copyright © 2025 Creative Arts Management OÜ
All rights reserved.

Author: Robert Ashford
ISBN HARDBACK: 978-1-80567-815-1
ISBN PAPERBACK: 978-1-80567-936-3

Starlight Circus

In a tent where comets prance,
Juggling stars in a cosmic dance.
Planets spin on a wobbly wire,
While black holes yawn with cosmic fire.

Galactic clowns with moonlit shoes,
Play pick-up sticks with giant blues.
Laughter echoes through the night,
As Martians juggle, what a sight!

Saturn's rings form a hula hoop,
As aliens form a hopping troupe.
A space raccoon steals some candy,
While space dust sparkles oh so dandy.

Join the show, don't miss the fun,
Underneath a neon sun.
This circus flies beyond the norm,
In a universe where quirks perform!

The Absurd Arrangement of the Universe

In this realm where nonsense thrives,
Quirky critters dance and jive.
A planet made of silly string,
To every whim, the universe will cling.

Stars wear hats, a mismatched lot,
Galaxies spin, a dizzying plot.
Black holes sneak in, funny surprises,
Swallowing jokes and strange disguises.

A sunbeam giggles, tickles the sky,
While moons play catch with a comet nearby.
Asteroids march in a conga line,
Singing tunes in a world divine.

Join the dance of the oddball fate,
Where every quirk helps us create.
Laughter echoes in endless sway,
In this mad creation, come what may!

Nightfall's Eccentricities

When night falls down like a warm hug,
Beneath the stars, a wacky rug.
Moonbeams twirl with a wink and grin,
As the universe lets the fun begin.

Shooting stars race like runaway cars,
While robots play chess with candy bars.
A cozy nebula brews tea with flair,
Inviting all to join in the rare.

A comet taps to a funky beat,
As stars on stilts dance with tiny feet.
Galactic critters in absurd attire,
Fueling their dreams with cosmic fire.

So dive into this whimsical spree,
Where every moment is wild and free.
Nightfall offers a laughter-filled flight,
In this playful dance of endless light!

The Cosmic Circus of Dreams

Welcome to a show beyond compare,
Where dreams take wing in cosmic air.
A cosmic ringmaster calls the scene,
With antics that make the laughter keen.

Clowns on meteors bounce and leap,
While starlit bears play hide and seek.
Astroids roll like oversized balls,
Sending giggles through the galaxy walls.

Dreams are woven in cotton candy haze,
As galaxies twirl in a dazzling maze.
Expect the weird and the wonderful cheer,
In a circus of laughs, stay near and dear.

So grab your ticket, take a seat,
To the curious beat of the universe's heartbeat.
In this funny realm where wonder streams,
Laughter is the root of all dreams!

Celestial Whims

In a galaxy of giggles, they dance so free,
Planets wear tutus, as bright as can be.
Stars throw confetti, in shades of lime,
Comets with ice cream, a treat so sublime.

Asteroids juggling, they tumble and spin,
While moons wear top hats, amused with a grin.
Saturn's rings sparkle, with bling in the night,
While space cats frolic, a whimsical sight.

A Dance of Peculiar Stars

Jupiter waltzes with a slip of the heel,
Venus does the cha-cha, in a cosmic reel.
Mars brings the rhythm, with a quirky beat,
While Neptune's the DJ, spinning tunes so sweet.

Pluto taps its foot, though it's quite far away,
Grinning mischievously, it joins the ballet.
Galaxies giggle, in a stellar swirl,
As cosmic confetti begins to unfurl.

Quirks in the Cosmos

Mercury's a prankster, full of surprise,
Flipping through space, with comical eyes.
Uranus does backflips, in a spiral of cheer,
While wild cosmic bunnies hop, never to fear.

A black hole takes selfies, with stars all around,
Collecting odd pictures, forever unbound.
The Milky Way chuckles, a grand theater bright,
Where oddities flourish, in pure delight.

Eccentric Paths

Each planet a character, with whimsical traits,
Dancing through stardust, they open the gates.
A comet with sneakers, races through space,
While the sun plays cards, with a bright smiling face.

In this cosmic circus, the giggles abound,
Where laughter echoes, a resonant sound.
Silly space creatures, with hats and with tails,
Stir up the cosmos, with zany tales.

Mysterious Luminaries

Balloons that dance with glee,
A fish that sings in a tree.
Under the moon's funny stare,
Socks and spoons float through the air.

Whispers from a purple cat,
Chasing shadows, where they sat.
Twirling hats that laugh and spin,
They join the game, let fun begin.

Glittering stars with silly grins,
Bubblegum dreams and chicken skins.
Juggling planets, how odd they seem,
Tickling the night with a chuckle and beam.

In this whimsical night sky,
Jellybeans bounce as clouds sigh.
Each twinkling light in a wacky dance,
Invites you now, come take a chance.

Wandering Through the Unusual

A teacup rides a rollercoaster,
With a giggle, it goes faster.
Lemonade falls like summer rain,
While daisies prance on a candy cane.

Upside down is where we roam,
Socks on heads feel just like home.
Jellyfish wear tiny hats,
Dancing with the bustling rats.

Elephants in sunglasses strut,
A turtle sings, 'What a nut!'
Pickles leap with all their might,
Wandering through this silly night.

In this land of twists and turns,
Laughter's flame brightly burns.
Join the parade, don't miss your cue,
In the unusual, we'll find the blue.

Echoes of the Eccentric

A trumpet's blast from a lengthened shoe,
Dandelions whisper secrets too.
Mirrored balloons reflect the sun,
Where the oddballs gather just for fun.

Beneath the stars that giggle and sway,
Cotton candy clouds dance in ballet.
Riddles crackle like fireflies bright,
Bringing joy to the sleeping night.

The moon wears glasses, a curious sight,
As taffy sticks tremble with delight.
Juggling spoons at the edge of time,
Echoes of laughter, a sweet little rhyme.

In a world where dreams collide,
Strawberry suns in cotton candy glide.
The eccentric's tune will always sing,
Join the magic, let your heart take wing.

Starlit Oddities

Jumping cats with neon hats,
Chasing echoes of silly chats.
Toffee comets streak through space,
While space ducks waddle with a grace.

Crispy crackers dance in pairs,
While jellybeans play musical stairs.
A pancake sings a morning tune,
Under the watch of a cheerful moon.

Sprinting brooms in a wild race,
Muffins giggle in their place.
Silly shapes bounce in delight,
Starlit oddities bright the night.

In this realm of quirky flair,
Wonders linger everywhere.
So let's embrace the fun tonight,
With laughter shining, burning bright.

The Exquisite Ballet of Oddities

In a cosmic dance with twirls so grand,
Aliens in tutus take a bold stand.
They pirouette near the purple suns,
While robots cheer, oh what fun runs!

Planets collide in a conga line,
Jellybeans raining, a sweet design.
A moonwalk performed by a quirky cat,
Tickling asteroids, imagine that!

Fantastic Folly among the Stars

Jupiter's juggling with a comet's tail,
While Martians giggle, they set sail.
Space clowns bounce on Saturn's rings,
Flipping pancakes, the joy it brings!

Neptune's winds play a funny tune,
As starfish dance with a giant spoon.
Aliens toast with fizzy drinks,
In zero G, where no one stinks!

The Enchantment of Erratic Paths

A twisting path through glittering skies,
Where goofy goblins wear silly ties.
They trip on stardust, laugh and roll,
In this strange realm, they steal the show.

Unicorns skydive without a care,
Landing softly on fluffy airborne chair.
Celestial cats chase meteors bright,
As shadows dance in the moonlit night.

Celestial Mischief

Meteors racing in wacky flights,
Chasing squirrels in sparkling lights.
Chimps with helmets spin and glide,
Through quirky dreams, they joyfully ride.

Galaxies giggle at the comets' play,
While space whales sing the blues all day.
A dodo bird counts the stars so high,
In this funny realm of up in the sky.

Fractured Light in the Milky Way

Stars twinkle with a giggle,
A comet trips on its tail,
Planets wear mismatched socks,
As the universe tells a tale.

Nebulas puff like old men,
Spilling colors everywhere,
Galactic clowns toss their hats,
Making laughter fill the air.

Black holes yawn with a flourish,
Swallowing light like it's cake,
Quasars dance in funny hats,
While the cosmos shakes and quakes.

The moon's a giant disco ball,
Reflecting dreams with a grin,
While meteors crack silly jokes,
As the night begins to spin.

The Mystique of Spinning Spheres

Jupiter plays hopscotch with Mars,
Swinging rings like a jump rope,
A cosmic ballet of oddities,
Where giggles leap and hope.

Saturn slides down rainbow trails,
With star dust stuck to its feet,
Venus winks from behind a cloud,
In a game that's quite discreet.

Pluto tries to join the fun,
But it's still an outer shy,
Dancing quietly in the dark,
While all the others fly high.

The sun bursts forth with a chuckle,
Flashing rays that tickle our skin,
In this realm of spinning spheres,
Life's a jest that must begin.

Cosmic Whimsy

Asteroids wear silly hats,
While flying by in a race,
Meteor showers rain down laughs,
In the vastness of space.

Galaxies swirl like twirling tops,
Creating chaos and cheer,
With aliens hosting tea parties,
It's out of this world, I hear.

Shooting stars grant goofy wishes,
As planets plot their next prank,
The universe loves a good laugh,
In its vast and glittering bank.

Every constellation's a riddle,
A puzzle wrapped in the night,
In this cosmic critter carnival,
Where everything's a delight.

The Uncharted Paths Above

A spaceship lost in a pizza slice,
Pizzas zoom, like they're alive,
Where funny creatures roam the stars,
And punchlines take a dive.

Silly squids float in zero-G,
Making faces at the sun,
While cosmic bubbles pop with glee,
Saying every day is fun.

Constellations tell funny stories,
As they stretch across the sky,
And every burst of stardust giggles,
As they laugh and wave goodbye.

On these paths of the undefined,
With each quirky twist and bend,
We find joy in every corner,
For the laughter never ends.

Planetary Paradox

In a world where socks are lost,
The sun plays tag with the moon.
Jupiter juggles big, bright balls,
While Martians dance to a tune.

Venus wears a purple hat,
Smelling like a giant cheese.
Saturn spins with silly rings,
While Mercury sneezes in the breeze.

Comets race on roller skates,
Leaving trails of sprinkles bright.
Asteroids throw dance parties,
Underneath the twinkling light.

Galaxies spin like tops,
While stars wear polka dots.
In this cosmic carnival,
Laughter fills the empty spots.

Surreal Revolutions

In a realm of upside-down,
Fish wear shoes and birds can drive.
Planets twirl in silly hats,
Pigs are flying, oh what a vibe!

Stars play chess with shooting rays,
While moons play hopscotch on the rings.
Galactic goo, a funny sight,
Makes light of cosmic things.

Gravity's lost its serious touch,
As rockets dance a jive.
Some planets blush in purple hues,
While others learn to thrive.

Space-time stretches like warm gum,
Creating worlds that make us grin.
In this madcap universal fun,
Silliness is bound to win.

Quasar Reveries

A quasar leaps in polka dots,
Winking at the nearest star.
It flings confetti through the void,
While gravity hums a bizarre guitar.

Neptune blew some bubble gum,
As Uranus danced on air.
The Milky Way lost its cool,
And twinkled without a care.

In this space of silly dreams,
Black holes laugh and sing a tune.
Galaxies spin like plates on sticks,
Creating a cosmic cartoon.

Eclipses wear the goofiest shades,
Shining with a grin so wide.
In this universe of laughter,
Even darkness can't hide.

The Astounding Carousel of Space

Round and round the planets spin,
On a merry-go-round of stars.
Asteroids ride the carousel,
While Venus strums her guitar.

Saturn sways with ribbons bright,
As comets zoom, a thrilling ride.
Galaxies whistle tunes of joy,
In this cosmic carnival guide.

The sun shines with a silly grin,
As moons do flips and tricks aplenty.
Nebulas swirl like cotton candy,
Making space feel warm and wavy.

Laughing meteors streak by fast,
In this game of cosmic chase.
Join the fun, don't miss out,
Life is a dance in outer space!

Eclipsed Oddities

A cat danced on the moonlit stage,
With shoes made of cheese, quite the rage.
Behind him a penguin, quite absurd,
Reciting in rhyme, though none heard.

The stars giggle, twinkle in delight,
As jellybeans rain down from great height.
An octopus juggles, what a sight!
While cows in the sky take their flight.

Gravity's Wondrous Disarray

A toaster flew past, toast in the air,
Causing a squirrel to stop and stare.
With gravity playing tricks on the day,
An elephant slicks down on a sleigh.

Around the corner, a llama skips,
Wearing a hat and flaunting its hips.
The laws of physics are far out of line,
As sparkly fish in the trees intertwine.

The Twilight Chronicles of Unusual Orbs

In twilight's grasp, the marbles roll,
Past dancing pickles with hearts of coal.
A fish on a skateboard with googly eyes,
Claims to discover the world's biggest pies.

The moon sneezes glitter, what a sound,
As cupcakes twirl in a merry round.
Giraffes in pajamas, oh what a thrill,
They brew silly potions with candy and chill.

Stardust Shenanigans

A kangaroo bounces across the sky,
With marshmallow clouds floating by.
A wizard spills soda, fizzing delight,
Making the universe seem out of sight.

Jellyfish glide on rollerblades swift,
Sharing their secrets, a bubbly gift.
Amidst the giggling stars, there's confusion,
As all join together for a cosmic fusion.

The Gravity of Unusual Things

In a land where socks wear shoes,
Flying cats play hopscotch, what a ruse.
Bananas groan in the sunlit shade,
While jellybeans in tuxedos wade.

A mustached fish rides a bicycle,
Twisting tales that are quite mythical.
Lemons argue with oversized pears,
As playful echoes fill the air.

Silly hats dance on a laughing breeze,
Tickled by whimsy, they tease and please.
A dog with glasses reads the news,
While squirrels debate the best kind of blues.

In the night, a mooncake sings a tune,
And marshmallows bounce under the cartoon.
Gravity's pull is a funny thing,
In this realm where oddities swing.

A Journey Beyond the Norm

Take a ride on a cake-shaped train,
Chasing shadows of purple rain.
Where spaghetti trees sway and sway,
And candy canes grow day by day.

Wombats wear tie-dye, wild and bold,
Reading stories of the quiet old.
Mermaids trade secrets with coral fish,
In this place where laughter's the wish.

Flying fish graze on starry dust,
Pigs on stilts add to the rust.
A round about with goofballs galore,
Each twist and turn opens a new door.

Backwards clocks tick in playful time,
Singing songs to a silly rhyme.
Join the journey, come one, come all,
In this realm where the oddities call.

Whirling Around the Extraordinary

Round and round, a merry-go-thing,
A chicken dressed up with a golden ring.
Twinkling teas serve a curious brew,
A flavor of laughter in every hue.

Cheese wheels race down the grassy hill,
While penguins try to perfect their thrill.
Zany ducks play hopscotch with flair,
How delightful, this quirky affair!

Up in the sky, a rainbow sneezes,
Sprinkling colors, oh, what it pleases.
A dragon on stilts rehearses its quip,
Chasing clouds with a playful dip.

Whirling and swirling, a whirlpool of fun,
In a world where weirdos get things done.
Join the dance, let the oddities shine,
In this topsy-turvy place, all is divine.

Uncommon Spheres

A roundabout of hamsters on wheels,
Zigzagging through gardens, a swirl of meals.
Octopuses juggling, it's quite a sight,
In the circus of quirks under moonlight.

Balloons with faces share silly jokes,
As penguins in bowties do handstands and pokes.
A toaster in a tutu leaps high and wide,
With a sprightly toaster cat at its side.

Upon a cloud, a fish takes a seat,
Counting the stars, oh, what a treat!
Where logic winks and laughter steals,
In quirky realms, nothing repeals.

With each odd step, the joy cascades,
Through these spheres where the humor invades.
Come dance along in the merry spree,
Where the unusual thrives, oh, can't you see?

Celestial Chronicles of the Unordinary

In the land of bright blue cheese,
Stars wear socks, if you please.
Planets juggle with delight,
Galaxies dance, oh what a sight!

Silly aliens sip their tea,
Bouncing high upon a tree.
Moonbeams giggle, how absurd,
As comets play a silly word.

Each asteroid tells a joke,
Nebulas puff and gently poke.
In this world where laughter sings,
Even black holes wear shiny rings.

So gather 'round, come join the fun,
In a universe where jokes are spun.
The stars are winking, can you see?
In this realm of pure glee!

The Lonesome Comet's Tale.

A comet travels, feeling blue,
No friends to chat with or pursue.
He drifts through space, a lonely plight,
Chasing stardust every night.

Then one day he spots a speck,
A fluffy cloud with quite a neck.
"Hello there!" cried the cloud with cheer,
"Want to giggle with me here?"

They danced beneath the sparkling stars,
Wearing hats made out of Mars.
So the comet laughed, then twirled about,
Together they giggled, without a doubt.

Now he flies with joy anew,
A colorful cloud and friend so true.
The lesson learned among the shake,
Friendship is the best star to make!

Celestial Curiosities

What's that floating? A purple frog!
Sipping tea on a cosmic log.
Planets with hats made of cosmic dust,
Laughing together, it's a must!

Meteorites hop in two-legged kicks,
Dancing in circles, pulling some tricks.
Saturn spins a tale so grand,
Jupiter's laughing, can you understand?

Stars trade jokes with a twinkling gleam,
Galactic squirrels work as a team.
They gather nuts from distant moons,
Singing silly yet catchy tunes.

In this sky where oddities thrive,
Funky friendships always arrive.
Join the laughter, don't miss the show,
In this universe, love will glow!

Whirlwind of Whims

A whirlwind spins with a zany twist,
Colors burst; you get the gist.
Shooting stars wear shades so bright,
Twinkling, winking, pure delight!

Comets ride on rainbow beams,
Chasing after chocolate dreams.
Asteroids play hopscotch on the way,
Finding gems on their silly stay.

Neptunes juggle water balloons,
Cackling madly, like silly loons.
The Milky Way sings a frothy tune,
As laughter echoes, life's a boon!

So let's spin, let's twirl and sway,
In this wacky, cosmic ballet.
With whimsical joy, we'll gleefully roam,
In this mad spiral we call home!

Cosmic Curiosities

In a galaxy of mismatched socks,
Planets dance in polka dots.
Meanwhile, the stars play peek-a-boo,
While comets slip on spacey shoes.

A unicorn in a UFO,
Bakes cookies made of starry dough.
Jellybeans float near Saturn's rings,
As a moon laughs and twirls and sings.

Green aliens juggle asteroids,
Cackling at their clumsy ploys.
A rubber chicken quacks and flies,
Underneath the cosmic skies.

With every quirk that makes us grin,
The universe spins in joyful spin.
Embrace the odd, let loose your glee,
In this wacky cosmic jamboree.

Spiral of the Surreal

In the nebula, a cat in shades,
Chasing meteors in playful parades.
Each twinkle whispers a silly clue,
As marshmallow asteroids drift on through.

Balloons made of stardust float,
While rubber ducks in spaceboats gloat.
A dancing space octopus sings,
Wearing a crown of glittery rings.

Cows with lasers fly past the moon,
In a funny, whimsical cartoon.
Galactic kittens yarn their way,
Through the surreal, come join the fray!

With laughter echoing through the night,
The cosmos beams, a splendid sight.
So spin in circles, let joy unfurl,
In this delightful, spiraled swirl.

The Unseen Side of Light

When shadows giggle and tickle the day,
Light dances above in a cheeky ballet.
A beam of laughter, bright and clear,
Wink at the darkness, spread the cheer.

In corners where stars begin to play,
Bouncing off walls in a funny way.
Mice in space with bright bow ties,
Throw a party as darkness flies.

Invisible squirrels ride on rays,
Making use of their cosmic plays.
A bubble of humor floats through bright,
Creating chuckles in every light.

So let's toast the joy that beams and shines,
Illuminate life with laughter's signs.
From the unseen to the very bright,
Embrace the wonders of joy and light.

Celestial Anomalies

In the sky, a fish rides a bike,
While penguins dressed as astronauts strike.
Planets spin on wobbly feet,
Shaking hands in this cosmic beat.

The sun tells jokes while sipping tea,
As satellites dance a jig with glee.
Margaritas served in star-shaped cups,
As aliens hiccup and hold their guts.

An octopus plays the cosmic flute,
Playing tunes that sound quite cute.
While rubber trees sway in the breeze,
Casting shadows that dance with ease.

Each quirk and twist disturbs the norm,
In this hilarious, galactic swarm.
So laugh with the stars, don't hold it tight,
In this realm of odd, pure delight!

Astral Oddballs

In the cosmos, where jesters dwell,
Stars play pranks, casting a spell.
Planets dance in silly attire,
Comets swirl like a wild choir.

Nebulas giggle, bright and bold,
While asteroids tell tales of old.
Wormholes wink, inviting you close,
In this circus, anything goes.

Galaxies twist, doing the jig,
Giant moons tease, doing a gig.
Rainbow rings whisper silly rhymes,
In this madness, we laugh through the times.

The Kaleidoscope Effect of the Infinite

Colors clash in a cosmic maze,
Lightbulbs flicker in puzzling ways.
A pink sun set with lime green clouds,
While laughter echoes, drawing crowds.

Planets sport hats, quite the sight,
With polka dots and stripes so bright.
Dancing comets with candy canes,
Silly antics hurt the brain!

Quasars giggle in rapid spins,
Supernovas wear the silliest grins.
In this jumbled scheme of delight,
The stars sparkle with sheer delight!

Proximity of Paradoxes

A cat in space wearing a tie,
Chasing lasers that zoom and fly.
Fish swim through the cosmic mist,
Sneaky shadows that can't resist.

A clock ticks backward, what a surprise,
Exploding penguins in the skies.
Chairs dance polka, socks hit the floor,
In this riddle, there's always more!

Frogs in tuxedos leap with flair,
While elephants float without a care.
Nonsense connects, interstellar wit,
In paradoxes, we never quit!

The Silly Symphony of Space

Planets strum their vibrant strings,
While meteors zap like rubber bands.
A symphony of giggles and chimes,
Echoes through starry paradigms.

Shooting stars slip on banana peels,
Comedic chaos, oh, how it appeals!
Space whales sing in jazzy tones,
While cheesy asides fill the zones.

Pianos float on clouds of fluff,
As rockets yell, 'This isn't tough!'
Microwaves hum in disharmony,
The jesters reign in cosmic glee!

Twilight of the Uncommon

In twilight's glow, a purple cow,
Dances with gnomes, oh, what a show!
A fish on a bike, it rides so fast,
While jellybeans rain, a sugary blast.

The trees wear hats, all tipped to one side,
As chickens in capes take a wild glide.
A dog plays chess, he's quite the whiz,
And all the frogs croak in a jazzy fizz.

A lizard with glasses reads the news,
While squirrels in suits sip on their brews.
The moon just chuckles at all the delight,
In this land of whimsy that twinkles at night.

Fantasia Among the Celestials

A comet with feathers skims through the void,
Spinning tops chase stars, oh, what a joy!
With lemons as suns in a berry-blue sky,
We dance on the rings as marshmallows fly.

A robot chef brews oddities galore,
With pickles and pudding, who could want more?
Gravity switches just for a laugh,
While purple pancakes stack in a path.

A giant snail races with nimble delight,
In slippers and shades, oh, what a sight!
The unicorns giggle, they leap and prance,
In a world where the strange always loves to dance.

The Strange Attraction

In a carnival tent shaped like a shoe,
A cactus plays guitar, yes, it's true!
With donuts as tickets, we spin and twirl,
While popcorn clouds make the world do a whirl.

A hamster in space boots runs a tall race,
Chasing a comet at a devilish pace.
Cotton candy planets drift lazily by,
As octopuses play drums, oh my, oh my!

Bubblegum comets burst into song,
With hidden surprises that never seem wrong.
A merry-go-round of the oddest design,
Where socks become friends, and all things align.

A Celestial Fable

In a realm where strange critters frolic and feed,
A penguin in pajamas plants magic seeds.
With every sprout grows a new kind of cheer,
As candy corn rainbows appear loud and clear.

The sun wears sunglasses, a quirky old chap,
While fireflies glow in a whimsical map.
A snail and a porcupine dance in the sand,
Creating a ruckus, oh, isn't it grand?

With chimps in ball gowns twirling about,
And cupcakes that giggle when they're taken out,
This fable unfolds with a comedic twist,
In a universe where oddities can't be missed.

The Laughter of Ancient Stars

In the sky where comets play,
Ancient stars giggle and sway.
They twinkle in such silly ways,
Chasing moons in cosmic frays.

Constellations trip and fall,
Making jokes with a cosmic call.
They dance around in silly cheer,
Making laughter ring so clear.

A supernova sneezes bright,
Throwing stardust in the night.
While black holes chuckle, spinning fast,
Swallowing laughter that won't last.

In this realm of joy untamed,
Even planets feel quite famed.
Galactic giggles fill the space,
In the warmth of light's embrace.

Unruly Galaxies

Galaxies whirl in wild delight,
Spinning round like kids in flight.
With stars that play hide and seek,
Their antics are truly unique.

Bouncing off dark matter's walls,
They tumble and giggle like tiny balls.
Whispering secrets in cosmic tones,
They poke fun at asteroids' moans.

Nebulas bloom in vibrant hues,
Wearing their colors like silly shoes.
With each flicker and flare they find,
They leave their giggles far behind.

In the chaos of stellar fun,
They twirl and shine like a warm sun.
These unruly formations roam,
Creating a universe that's like home.

Whimsical Wavelengths

Wavelengths dance with quirky grace,
Tickling light in a curious space.
They wiggle and squirm without a care,
Singing tunes that bounce in air.

From radio waves to cosmic rays,
They chirp and giggle in funny ways.
In each flicker, a joke is spun,
Turning light into playful fun.

Gravity waves jump with flair,
Creating ripples everywhere.
They snicker softly in the void,
Making physics a game enjoyed.

In this theater of zany light,
Stars perform their best at night.
With every twirl and every quip,
The universe shares in this raucous trip.

The Frivolous Galaxy

A frivolous galaxy spins so wide,
Where stars and planets take a ride.
They wear their hats and silly shoes,
Creating a scene you can't refuse.

Asteroids roll like bumpy stones,
Singing a tune in comical tones.
While comets race with tails that swirl,
In this cosmic dance, they whirl and twirl.

In the midst of this cosmic spree,
Photon giggles float so free.
Meteors dart with a wink and sigh,
Giggling as they zoom on by.

With laughter lost in the starlit hugs,
The universe hums with joyous shrugs.
In this goofy, cheerful spree,
Even light embraces its glee.

The Baffling Beauty Above

Up in the sky, a green fish flies,
Wearing a cape, much to our surprise.
Singing a tune, oh what a sight,
Dancing with clouds, through day and night.

A cat with a hat, on a bicycle rides,
Chasing a mouse, it cheerfully glides.
The moon cracks a joke, in a giggly way,
While stars laugh on cue, and join the play.

Twilight Tales of the Unsung

A rabbit in slippers, sipping some tea,
Tells tales of the cosmos, just for me.
With stars as his audience, quite astounded,
Each story he spins, with laughter is bounded.

An octopus juggles, with seven bright balls,
Doing the cha-cha, behind cosmic walls.
The comets all cheer, with a glittering cheer,
As twilight unfolds, it's the best time of year.

Stars in Chaotic Harmony

The sun wears glasses, playing it cool,
While planets are prancing, about the school.
A dog in a tux, does a waltz in the sky,
Spinning in circles, oh my, oh my!

A llama in space, with balloons on its back,
Shows off its tricks, in a cosmic attack.
As meteors tumble, and stars take a bow,
Life's such a hoot, here, take a look now!

The Marvelous Menagerie Above

There's a penguin in boots, running a stand,
Selling ice cream, it's totally planned.
With flavors like comet, or bubble wrap cheer,
The taste of the stars, always draws near.

A squirrel with a tie, reads newspapers to crows,
While giraffes in pajamas, swap tales as it snows.
Each critter has quirks, it's a whimsical spree,
In the dazzling heights, of our galaxy free.

Mysterious Paths of Celestial Bodies

There's a comet that giggles, a star that sneezes,
Planets wear socks while the universe teases.
A moon in a tutu, dancing with glee,
Suns popping bubbles in zero-gravity.

Gravity's laughing, it trips on its shoes,
While asteroids play hopscotch with bright-hued blues.
Neptune juggles raindrops like weird little clowns,
While Saturn spins plates, painting smiles for towns.

Jupiter's painting, with delight in its eye,
A canvas of laughter hangs up in the sky.
Martian ants are marching, with hats on their heads,
While Venus eats pizza on soft fluffy beds.

So up in the heavens, a revelry swirls,
Each quirk and each oddity, dancing in twirls.
Bring out the confetti, it's time for a show,
In this cosmic circus, let the good times flow.

The Peculiar Waltz of Planets

In a waltz of the weird, the planets align,
With Mercury giggling, it sips on moonshine.
Venus in polka dots starts doing the twist,
While Earth brings the rhythm that none can resist.

Mars with its maracas, shaking with flair,
Jupiter joins in with an extravagant air.
With Pluto now leading in sneakers so bright,
Even the comets are twirling at night.

A dance of the cosmic, a rollicking spree,
Galactic choreography, wild as can be.
Stars flash their skirts in a dazzling spin,
While black holes just giggle, waiting to win.

With laughter and music, the Milky Way spins,
Nothing too serious, just whimsical grins.
The planets frolic, in joyous parade,
As the universe chuckles at all that we've made.

Bizarre Fantasia in the Sky

Once in a sky where the quirky reside,
Clouds crack up laughing, so silly and wide.
A whale on a rocket, it splashes through stars,
While UFOs play tag with Martian guitars.

A dragon in pajamas zips past with a cheer,
Shooting out sparkles that tickle the sphere.
Every star's a wink, every planet a jest,
As laughter erupts from the universe's vest.

Moons wear top hats and perform with delight,
While shadows do cartwheels, oh what a sight!
Constellations chuckle their mischief aloud,
Creating a ruckus, enthralling the crowd.

Then rainbow meteors dive, take a spin,
Wobbling through laughter, inviting us in.
In this bizarre show, where oddities play,
The sky is a stage, come join the ballet.

Twisted Constellations

Among the stars, where oddities bloom,
Twisted constellations make room for the boom.
One throws a pie while another takes flight,
Chasing the moonbeams with sheer delight.

A horse with four wings flies upside down,
While kittens in goggles play hopscotch in town.
Shooting stars giggle, tickling the night,
As they pass by the dwellers of cosmic light.

A bear in a sombrero jiggles and spins,
As aliens dance with inelegant grins.
They gather around as the planets all cheer,
In this heavenly circus, there's nothing to fear.

With laughter and whimsy, the twilight ignites,
Creating a carnival of brilliant sights.
So come take a peek, at this nonsense we find,
In the wondrous expanse, let imagination unwind.

Luminous Oddities in Motion

Silly stars in hats so bright,
They trip and tumble every night.
With comets racing through the sky,
They laugh and wink as they zoom by.

Asteroids in roller skates,
Spinning round and dodging fates.
Jupiter's got a dancing spree,
While Saturn spins with glee, whee!

Giggles bounce on solar winds,
While cheeky moons play hide and seek.
A galaxy of goofy friends,
Join this cosmic sneak peek.

So grab your cap and join the fun,
The party starts when day is done.
With every twirl and silly twist,
You won't want to be missed!

Ecliptic Reverberations

In circles round, the planets play,
Their funny tricks light up the day.
A waltz of moons and suns so bright,
Creating giggles in the night.

Neptune spins on pogo sticks,
While Mars invents weird magic tricks.
Venus jogs with flashy shoes,
Avoiding space dust and cosmic blues.

Zany aliens set the beat,
Dancing with their tiny feet.
In this realm of comedy,
The stars are all too proud to see.

And in this dance of endless glee,
We float along so wild and free.
Each pulse of light a laugh resounds,
In this crazy cosmic playground!

The Daring Dances of Cosmic Forms

Look at Pluto twirl in place,
With a tutu made of stardust lace.
Uranus does the hula hoop,
While meteors just laugh and droop.

Asteroids in pairs do tango,
With comets joining the fandango.
The Milky Way's a disco floor,
Where galactic grooves outpour.

A quasar leads a jazzy tune,
While moons all gather, hum, and croon.
The sun spins like a disco ball,
Reflecting joy upon us all.

So let's keep dancing, never stop,
In this universe, we love to hop.
With laughter echoing through the space,
Join this fun-filled, cosmic race!

Supernova Shenanigans

Supernova bursts and fireworks loud,
Stars are laughing, it's a cosmic crowd.
Black holes giggle, pulling tight,
Swirling worlds disappear from sight.

Planets play peek-a-boo all day,
Popping up in the Milky Way.
Galaxies twirl in a merry chase,
Creating smiles, lighting up space.

Cosmic balloons float up so high,
As aliens bake a pie in the sky.
With sprinkles of starlight, it looks divine,
Let's gather 'round and share some wine!

So when the night glimmers with light,
Remember this party, oh what a sight!
In this playground of stars so bright,
The fun never ends, it's pure delight!

Dancing with Driftwood Stars

Beneath a sky of scattered twigs,
The stars perform their clumsy gigs.
A moonbeam slips on a dancing shoe,
And puddles giggle in the view.

With each spin, a seagull cries,
A riddle wrapped in burnt-up pies.
The constellations chuckle aloud,
While driftwood winks, part of the crowd.

A comet trips on a tangle of reeds,
Singing songs of bizarre misdeeds.
Galaxies trade their silliest tales,
While sandcastles dodge faint gales.

So dance with me, amidst the trees,
Where starfish hum and the breeze agrees.
In this quirky, whimsical place,
Even the sky has a goofy face.

Echoes of the Unseen

In a realm of giggles and peeks,
Where shadows tickle and the gigglers speak,
Invisible hiccups ripple like waves,
As lighthearted whispers dance in caves.

A rainbow prisms to laugh with glee,
Poking fun at the unwelcome bee.
While wishes bounce like rubber balls,
And laughter echoes off marble walls.

The moon sneezes with a silvery flare,
Leaving comets scratching at air.
In the jokes of the night, no one fears,
For madness fades, and mirth appears.

So listen close to the unseen sounds,
Where humor skips over grassy grounds.
Let the echoes tickle your very core,
And leave you longing for even more.

Whirling Whims of the Heavens

Up in the tapestry of the sky,
Clouds throw pie fights, oh my, oh my!
With marshmallow puffs and blueberry tart,
The sun shades itself, a work of art.

Planets prance with an awkward grace,
In a cosmic three-legged race.
A starlight breeze teases the moon,
While wishing stars whistle a silly tune.

Asteroids juggle their rocky friends,
While the universe giggles, never ends.
Nebulas spin like dizzy tops,
In a carnival where hilarity hops.

Join the dance of whimsical days,
Where lightheartedness sprawls and plays.
For up above, the skies are bright,
Full of chuckles that take flight.

Celestial Mirth

In the pocket of the sky so wide,
Chortles bounce like a starry ride.
Galaxies roll their giggly eyes,
While comets chase fireflies.

Whimsical waves of cosmic cheese,
Float on stardust, breezy and free.
Each twinkle holds a secret joke,
That even the dark cannot revoke.

Clouds in tutus flit and sway,
Ballet of light on display.
A universe painted with laughter's brush,
Turns silence into a joyous rush.

So revel in this playful view,
Where celestial beings know what to do.
For mirth is the fuel for stars so bright,
In the dance of joy, they ignite the night.

Celestial Bloom of the Unusual

In a garden where stars grow bright,
A potato dressed in quirky light.
Dancing moons with mismatched shoes,
Comet kites spread silly views.

Marshmallow clouds in the sky,
Jellybean trees that wave goodbye.
A rabbit in a top hat grins,
On a roller coaster made of pins.

Planets juggle, stars throw pies,
Worms in tuxedos start to rise.
Chasing dreams on a rainbow slide,
While unicorns take a silly ride.

Gears of laughter spin around,
In this place, joy can be found.
With every hop and twist, delight,
In peculiar blooms, we take flight.

Starlit Surrealism

Under stars with hats and quirks,
Dancing squirrels do crazy works.
Guitars made of moonbeams strum,
As jellyfish play the beating drum.

Clouds flip-flop in a whimsical way,
While candy canes join the fray.
A cosmic clown leaps with grace,
In a world of laughter, we embrace.

Pulsing lights in a pixelated waltz,
Synchronized with every pulse.
Painted skies of emerald green,
Reveal a circus, grand and keen.

Whimsical thoughts take flight and twirl,
In the laughter, we swirl and whirl.
With each joke from distant stars,
Life is but a blaze of bizarre.

Gravity's Playground of Wonders

On a swing hung from a comet's tail,
Jumping high without a fail.
Giggles echo beneath the sun,
In the playground, oh what fun!

With slides made of twinkling beams,
And merry-go-rounds of candy dreams.
Where alien kids play hopscotch wide,
As bubbles float and dreams collide.

Levels change with every laugh,
In this world, we find our path.
A trampoline made of starry light,
Bouncing higher, what a sight!

Giggling critters roll and glide,
As we frolic, side by side.
In this haven, joy is found,
Where wonders dance and hearts rebound.

Prismed Realities

Through the glass of a rainbow hue,
Odd things pop out, just for you.
A fish that rides a unicycle,
Makes us giggle for a while.

With zebras that wear polka dots,
And jumping frogs in funny spots.
Mirrored smiles in quirky frames,
Earth spins with its whimsical games.

A toast from squirrels in tuxedos,
Toasting to all the playful videos.
In this realm of vivid delight,
Every shadow dances, takes flight.

Bright confetti falls from space,
Painting laughter on every face.
In visions strange, we cheer and play,
In a world that's funny, come what may!

Wondrous Whirls in the Dark

In the night, the stars dance bright,
A cow in a tutu, what a sight!
Juggling planets, so silly and bold,
Galaxies laugh, their secrets unfold.

A comet slips on a banana peel,
Spinning like mad, what a fun reel!
Aliens giggle, they roll on the floor,
With popcorn in space, who could ask for more?

Asteroids wear hats, oh what a scene,
Swirling around in a cosmic routine.
The moon makes a face, such a funny guy,
Winking at Earth as he waves goodbye.

Every night's party, a delightful spree,
Where the weirdest of beings are wild and free.
Join in the fun, give a spin with glee,
In this universe, where whimsy's the key!

The Riddle of Celestial Choreography

Under twinkling lights, a dance takes flight,
Jellybeans twirl, pure delight!
Mars wears a tutu, full of flair,
While Saturn just laughs, with rings in the air.

Shooting stars play tag, what a fray,
With space cows grazing, munching away.
Planets giggle, they trip and slide,
On stardust paths, their silly ride.

A space whale sings a ludicrous tune,
Chasing comets around the moon.
Is that a UFO wearing a hat?
Oh yes it is, imagine that!

Throw in some meteors, wear a bright mask,
Watch them boogie, what a fun task!
In this playful ballet, joy knows no bound,
With laughter and chaos, happiness found!

Astounding Attitudes of the Firmament

In a realm where the bizarres convene,
Stars play poker, it's quite the scene!
Neptune's the dealer, with eight eyes wide,
Jupiter's bluffing, can't keep it inside.

Rockets wear sneakers, run laps in the void,
While glittering quasars feel overjoyed.
Uranus tells jokes, or so they say,
But no one can see him, he's hiding away!

Galactic pranks with a slapstick twist,
Nebulas jest, no way to resist!
A black hole's punchline—oh, it's so trite,
But laughter erupts in the cold, dark night.

When the constellations come out to play,
They whir up a party, hip-hip-hooray!
With each cosmic chuckle, the planets align,
In this ridiculous spectacle, all is just fine!

Spaceships of the Irregular

In the galaxy far, aboard a strange ship,
A penguin navigates with a silly flip.
He steers with a fish, quite the odd sight,
As asteroids cheer under the starlight.

Squids in a band belt out cosmic tunes,
While robots do the twist under the moons.
Laughter erupts as they spin and glide,
In this mismatched crew, there's nowhere to hide!

Wobbling rockets, they bounce and sway,
Sailing through stardust, oh what a play!
With jelly on board, they fuel up with glee,
In spaceships of oddness, they're truly free.

Each journey a jest, in this cosmic lane,
Where laughter ignites and banter's the game.
Through nebulae bright, with joy they soar,
Here in the universe, adventure's a roar!

The Outlandish Flicker

In a realm where socks refuse to pair,
A dance of dust bunnies fills the air.
Cats wear hats and dogs play the lute,
While squirrels juggle and chase a hoot.

Turtles race on skateboards with flair,
Pigeons debate in the town square.
A frog in a tux sips tea with grace,
As crickets critique the latest base.

A fish sings jazz from a bubble bath,
While bees crack jokes that make you laugh.
The moon takes photos, it's quite the scene,
Of silly shadows dancing on green.

With each twinkle, odd tales arise,
Like unicorns trading in their fries.
In this place where silliness is key,
Laughter reigns—come join the spree!

Fables of the Whimsical

There once was a cow with a polka-dot coat,
Who dreamed of sailing on a bright pink boat.
She paddled with pigeons, her loyal crew,
As they searched for the land of the bubblegum dew.

A wise old wallaby played jazz on a tree,
While kangaroos danced, oh so carefree.
The moon chuckled softly at the joyful spree,
As jellybeans rained down in glee.

A bear in a bowtie ran a sweet café,
Where cookies and giggles were served every day.
With each silly story, a giggle would bloom,
In the land where odd fables resume.

The owls told tales 'til the sun peeked out,
Of dancing giraffes and a cake made of clout.
In this world of whimsy, all dreams intertwine,
Every odd little moment, oh how they shine!

Luminescent Oddities

In a meadow where sunlight plays peek-a-boo,
Daisies wear sunglasses, a stylish crew.
The grass tickles toes as the breeze spins round,
While butterflies giggle, their joy profound.

A trampoline shop run by cheeky wee mice,
Became quite the hub sprinkled with spice.
Jelly jars bouncing down the hill with ease,
Splat! A berry burst, sticky arms get squeezed.

A frog in a tutu rips the dance floor,
While llamas in bowties groan for encore.
The stars above laugh, winking bright,
Wishing for whirls of oddball delight.

As laughter erupts like a fizzy balloon,
A dragon whispers jokes to the noon.
In this luminous land of peculiar cheer,
Every oddity twinkles, bringing us near!

A Galaxy of Oddball Dreams

In a galaxy where spoons wear shoes,
And stars sit in chairs sipping bright blue brews.
Planets play tag in a whimsical swirl,
While comets share secrets with a frizzy whirl.

A clever old cat spun yarns made of light,
As meteors danced on this magical night.
Through stardust and giggles, the creatures weep,
For funny little dreams never stop to sleep.

A parade of oddities in colorful hues,
Where jellyfish giggle, and snails sing the blues.
In this realm full of laughter, all worries dissolve,
While curious stars spin in the cosmic revolve.

With quirky companions in a faraway space,
Frogs on unicycles run a wild race.
In a galaxy bright with oddball schemes,
Every moment is painted with laughter and dreams!

Gravity's Anomalous Embrace

A cat in a hat flies high with glee,
While toasters toast bread in flight, you see.
Juggling pickles, a clown takes a chance,
As rubber ducks waltz in a cosmic dance.

Socks in the dryer make quite the scene,
Swirling in spins like a washing machine.
Here, laughter erupts from a bouncing frog,
Chasing a snail on a log made of fog.

Dragons sip tea in a world made of cheese,
While unicorns stroll under ticklish trees.
The skies turn to giggles; stars sparkle bright,
In this zany delight, oh, what a sight!

With crayons as comets, coloring space,
Drawing chuckles that dance and embrace.
In this quirky realm where nonsense prevails,
The beauty of weirdness forever exails.

Whimsical Trajectories

Penguins in polka dots fly in a line,
Slipping on saturns like slips of fine wine.
A llama in sandals runs circles around,
Spinning in laughter, feels joy unbound.

Flying fish giggle as they bounce off the moon,
Making confetti from bubbles that swoon.
Kangaroos skip with their pockets so wide,
Holding the secrets that space tries to hide.

Silly mice dance in their oversized shoes,
While giraffes juggling moonbeams spread news.
Asteroids waltz with a rhythm so slick,
As planets play leapfrog with a bounce and a kick.

When clowns in the cosmos make rocket balloon,
A festival happens under the bright noon.
In this playful space where joy never ends,
Giggles unite as the universe bends.

The Uncharted Sky

A fish in a bowl dreams of wandering far,
As squirrels in capes fly from star to star.
Waffles in orbit sing songs on their way,
With syrupy giggles that sweeten the day.

A teapot in flight brews a laughter-filled brew,
While owls in tuxedos conspire with a crew.
Jumping on clouds, they play hide and seek,
In a world where the odd is the prime mystique.

Rainbow-hued hippos float high in the breeze,
Dancing on bubbles that float like the seas.
Parrots recite poetry upside down,
As the jester of time wears a comical crown.

With jellybean planets and marshmallow stars,
Every giggle expands like the galaxies are.
In this uncharted sky, we laugh till we're sore,
For the universe's quirks ignite joy evermore.

Paradoxical Patterns

A clock made of pasta counts minutes in sauce,
As cabbage patch kids spin like a boss.
While waffles in shirts do a jive on a rail,
Pretzels declare they will never fail.

A bicycle flies with its wheels all aglow,
Toot after toot, it puts on quite a show.
The cat with a monocle sips tea with delight,
As jellybeans pirouette into the night.

The moon wears a tutu; the stars laugh aloud,
In this place where the silly is ever so proud.
Chickens in top hats make speeches so grand,
While marshmallows jump to take the main stand.

In this twisty domain of whimsical cheer,
Oddities gather, and laughter draws near.
Each paradox shines with a humorous gleam,
As reality dances within a sweet dream.

Anomalous Secrets of the Cosmos

In a galaxy where cats wear hats,
And dogs do waltzes with acrobats.
Stars giggle as they twinkle bright,
While comets play hide and seek at night.

Planets spin in a silly dance,
Jupiter trips, and Saturn prances.
Nebulas puff like cotton candy,
While black holes snack on stars so dandy.

Aliens brew their cosmic stew,
With flavors strange and colors blue.
They chuckle as they sip their drink,
While meteor showers make them blink.

In this realm of whimsical sights,
Laughter echoes in dazzling flights.
The universe sings a joyful song,
In chaotic mirth, where all belong.

Celestial Mavericks

Comets wear sunglasses, lookin' fly,
As they zoom past with a cheeky cry.
Mars cracks jokes to the moons in tow,
While asteroids tumble, putting on a show.

Neptune's blue is quite the tease,
While aliens play tag with the cosmic breeze.
Shooting stars wink as they swoosh by,
In this carnival where dreams can fly!

Black holes open wide, watch their grin,
As they gobble up laughter and spin.
The cosmos giggles, what a sight,
In this maverick dance, pure delight!

Galaxies swirling in perfect queues,
Tickle the giants with glittery shoes.
Bizarre adventures await everyone,
In this universe of silly fun!

Galactic Jesters

In the stellar court, jesters play,
With rubber chicken stars on display.
Jupiter howls with laughter loud,
As aliens dance in a big, bright crowd.

Uranus cracks a pun so sly,
While meteors fall, oh me, oh my!
Pluto jokes about being small,
Yet his charm makes him stand tall.

Supernovas pop like party balloons,
While quasars hum a tune about loons.
Cosmic clowns juggle dark matter too,
In this endless carnival, just for you!

Stars take turns with their best routines,
Eclipses peek behind the scenes.
With giggles echoing through the void,
This jesters' realm cannot be destroyed.

The Comedy of Cosmic Uncertainty

Planets wobble in a ridiculous way,
As space-time throws them a quirky play.
Galaxies spin, but who knows why?
With every twist, they giggle and sigh.

Asteroids argue over their course,
While meteoric mishaps create discourse.
Saturn slips on its own ring,
Much to the laughter of everything.

Time travelers trip on their own feet,
In a race with stars that never meet.
Wormholes fumble, making a scene,
In this cosmic show that feels so keen.

Eclipses wink with a playful tease,
While cosmic winds dance with such ease.
In each oddity, humor unfolds,
In this grand tale that never gets old.

The Eccentric Dance of Stars

Stars in tutus spin around,
The comets blushing, feeling proud.
With a twirl, the planets prance,
In the night, they take their chance.

They giggle as they twinkle bright,
Winking at us from their height.
Meteor showers laugh and play,
Shooting puns that drift away.

Black holes wear a silly hat,
Swirling in a cosmic spat.
Gravity's the punchline here,
As galaxies jump, shout, and cheer.

In this dance of cosmic glee,
No one's quite what they seem to be.
Join the stars in their bizarre show,
Where the oddities freely glow.

Enigma in the Galaxy

In the depths where mysteries rife,
Aliens juggle with their life.
They balance jokes on tiny beams,
Crafting laughter from wild dreams.

Planets play hide and seek all day,
Saturn's rings, they lead astray.
"Catch me if you can!" they tease,
As crab nebula spins with ease.

Each star sparkles with a grin,
While black holes chuckle from within.
A cosmic riddle in the mix,
Makes even time do silly tricks.

Floating in this stellar spree,
Where each moment's pure jubilee,
The galaxy sings a silly tune,
Dancing wildly 'neath the moon.

Outlandish Trails of Light

Zipping comets race and laugh,
Leaving trails like silly gaff.
Each twinkle tells a funny tale,
Where space itself begins to ail.

Asteroids form a rock 'n' roll band,
With beats that shake the sleepy sand.
They jam across the cosmic waves,
Dancing like a bunch of knaves.

Neutron stars wear mismatched shoes,
In colors that no one would choose.
They prance around in boisterous cheer,
Creating tunes that all can hear.

Through the chaos and the flare,
Are moments woven with great care.
Light years travel just for fun,
In this wacky place, we all won.

Cosmic Quirks Unraveled

Planets wear the silliest hats,
While suns host tea with funny cats.
The constellations wink and jive,
In a space where oddballs thrive.

Pulsars blink with cheeky signs,
As galaxies draw doodled lines.
They scribble jokes in cosmic dust,
A reminder that in stars we trust.

Each quirk is part of the grand show,
Where light years dance and radiate glow.
Through the nebula's misty schemes,
Are hidden giggles, bright as dreams.

In the end, it's one big laugh,
As asteroids make a cartoon path.
So come join the celestial spree,
And dance beneath the cosmic tree.

Curved Lights and Echoes

A banana spins in space, full of glee,
While socks dance around a cosmic tree.
Jupiter giggles, wearing a starry hat,
While Pluto wonders where his shoes are at.

Comets swirl like noodles in a bowl,
Asteroids playing tag, it's a funny goal.
Galaxies twirl in a wacky waltz,
Stars whisper jokes that cause light to pulse.

A rubber chicken lands on Mars's sand,
Sending ripples across the silent land.
Rings of Saturn, like hoops in a game,
Laugh out loud, but who's to blame?

With every twinkle, a chuckle is shared,
In this wild theater, nobody's scared.
A cosmic circus full of delight,
Where oddities shimmer in the night.

The Peculiarness of Celestial Patterns

Stars wear pajamas in a silly way,
While moons do the cha-cha come what may.
Mercury sips tea, takes a tiny break,
Saying, 'Life in space is no piece of cake!'

Dancing meteors leave a dazzling trace,
While planets giggle in a crowded space.
Cosmic painters splash colors so bright,
Creating laughter on the canvas of night.

A spaceship disguised as a giant shoe,
Zooms past the comets, it's quite the view.
Alien children play leapfrog on stars,
Giggling together, they've come from afar.

Constellations rearranging their shapes,
Making funny faces, who needs landscapes?
In this bizarre sky where wonder abounds,
The peculiar patterns make joyful sounds.

Cosmic Carnival of Curiosities

At the fair of the stars, the rides spin fast,
With cotton candy clouds, a whimsical blast.
Popcorn comets pop with a sizzle and cheer,
As laughter echoes across the frontier.

A merry-go-round made of glittery light,
Where meteors loop and dance through the night.
Space clowns juggle planets with ease and flair,
While rockets fire confetti in the air.

The ring toss is tricky, it's asteroids galore,
Win yourself a black hole from the cosmic store.
Silly signs read, "No gravity allowed!",
Bringing forth giggles from the floating crowd.

Underneath starlight, adventures unfold,
In this carnival where weird tales are told.
A festival bursting with laughter and fun,
In celestial realms, we've only begun.

The Phantasmagorical Night Sky

The night sky grins with a wobbly face,
As clowns on comets frolic through space.
Nebulas chuckle, with colors so bright,
Painting a canvas full of delight.

Saturn's rings swing in an elegant dance,
While actors in stars take a chance.
A purple cow moons under the glow,
As magic unfolds in the celestial show.

Black holes burst out laughing, tickling light,
Spinning tales of whimsy in the cool night.
The sun in pajamas peeks from the east,
Excited to join in this oddball feast.

Wishing on stars that tumble and sway,
Creating silly dreams that linger and play.
In this phantasmagorical night up above,
Wonder and giggles are what we all love.

www.ingramcontent.com/pod-product-compliance
Lightning Source LLC
Chambersburg PA
CBHW051644160426
43209CB00004B/787